"While most dance students have drea es
life in dance involves, they are often t es
of this professional life once they beg ed
that *Dance Life* will help to put their e
these realities and assist them in more ...., pirparing for their
lives in dance after they leave school as full time students."

Mavis Staines
Artistic Director/Ballet Principal
The National Ballet School of Canada

"We are living in a period of change; almost the whole world is in
transition. This manual will become the definite "bible" for the young
artist who needs to get in touch with the professional realities of the
dance world."

Peter Boneham
Artistic Director
Le Groupe de la Place Royal

"Mr. Pearl's book provides young aspiring artists with recognition and
validation for their struggles. It includes a great number of helpful
suggestions and activities to guide these young dancers towards a
healthy attitude and sense of community. This book is empowering
and long overdue."

Tom Stroud
Artistic Director
Contemporary Dancers Inc.

". . . a wonderful, moving document for professional dance students.
It is wise, generous, deep and witty. I love it and can't wait to use it."

Billyann Balay
Principal (1989)
School of the Toronto Dance Theatre

"Finally someone who had similar questions and worries as me, gave
me the means to figure out solutions. It's realistic and positive. The
entire book was a big help."

Student
The School of the Toronto Dance Theatre

DANCE LIFE

Kenny Pearl

Canadian Cataloguing in Publication Data

Pearl, Kenny, date -
Dance life

Issued also in French under title: Une vie de danse.
ISBN 0-9698273-0-X

1. Dancing - Vocational guidance. I. Dancer Transition
Centre. II. Title.

GV1597.P4 1994   792.8'023   C94-931109-X

A major portion of the proceeds from this book will go to the Dancer
Transition Centre who commissioned it.

The Dancer Transition Centre gratefully acknowledges the funding of
this project by:

The Canada Council, Dance Section
Ontario Arts Council, Dance Section
The Secretary of State of Canada, Promotion of Official Languages
Branch.

The Dancer Transition Centre would also like to acknowledge the
following people for their assistance:

Maureen Consolati - editing
Rea Wilmshurst - editing

Maryvon Delanoë - translation

The Dancer Transition Centre wishes finally to thank McClelland &
Stewart, *The Canadian Publishers*, for its help in the design and
production of this book.

Table of Contents

introduction

T he main purpose of this book is to give you tools that you can use to explore your life in and out of dance, tools that will help you deal fully and positively with many of the possibilities a life in dance has to offer. Your interaction with the material over the year will lead to discoveries that can take much of the confusion out of your transition from full-time student to professional dancer.

If you give it some time, the material will help you expand your point of view, making you increasingly aware of the way your profession relates to the world in which you live and of your place in the history of your own life, with a past that affects your present and a future that depends very much for its shape on the choices you make — and must know you can make — now.

These are very grand goals. But right from the beginning they must be so, because you have expressed a need for information and you deserve support.

Some of the issues presented involve exploring feelings of self-worth and how they affect your life, developing depth and range as an artist and clearing up misinformation as to what professional life involves.

To get the most out of this material, you will have to take some risks — by exploring your own personal history, sharing your insights and being open enough to give and accept feedback.

There are many forms of dance and many people dancing in most countries around the world. There are traditions in dance in some cultures that go back much farther than the beginnings of dance in the western world. This book was written primarily to address concerns of students training in the disciplines of modern dance and ballet.

The Dancer Transition Centre

The Dancer Transition Centre is a Canadian organization that provides moral, advisory and financial support in assisting professional dancers during their transition from actively performing to second careers. It also operates as a resource centre for the dance community and the general public by providing free seminars, educational materials and information. It is centred in Toronto, with branches in Ottawa, Montreal, Quebec City, Winnipeg, Vancouver and Edmonton.

The Centre was founded by Joysanne Sidimus, who has had an international career as a dancer, teacher and rehearsal director, performing with companies that include The National Ballet of Canada, New York City Ballet and London's Festival Ballet. She has been involved with the issue of career transition since 1981, when she started researching the subject for her book *Exchanges, Life After Dance.*

Convinced of the need for a service to aid the retiring dancer, Joysanne founded and now is executive director of the Dancer Transition Centre. The very-active president of the Dancer Transition Centre is Karen Kain, internationally renowned principal dancer with The National Ballet of Canada.

So why is the Centre concerned with students?

You are just about to get started on a career as a professional dancer. But at the same time you're retiring as a full-time dance student. The transition you will soon be making and probably are already thinking about can cause as much confusion as any other.

After holding many seminars with students in a number of professional schools, Joysanne realized that if given a forum in which to speak out, dance students often exploded with emotion concerning their doubts and fears about their progress and the change in their lives that is quickly approaching.

They expressed their confusion in such statements as:

"I feel exposed and shaky — on the verge of explosion. It's my whole life to be here, but I'm confused."

"Dealing positively with my frustrations and insecurities is my most difficult task.... Will I or will I not keep finding the strength to go on with this struggle?"

Dancers who feel this way need help to deal with their confusion. Right from the beginning, it is important to say that confusion is not necessarily bad. It is natural for any process of transformation and growth to include times of self-doubt as perceptions change and as new lessons are learned. Confusion can be a healthy stage of an ongoing process, as long as it is part of the process and not an enduring state encouraged by misinformation.

First of all, getting through all the trials and difficulties of a professional school deserves top marks. The transition ahead will take you into a world of much fulfillment, but also one in which you will have to keep your heart, mind, body and spirit in balance under what will be some difficult circumstances.

Secondly, many former dancers have expressed the feeling that if only they had thought about and done "certain things" while they were still dancing, their careers probably would have been longer and richer. Extending and enriching a life in dance are very good reasons for a little extra thinking and doing.

This book will give you a framework of support as you make this big transition in your life. But because, ultimately, you and only you are responsible for your own life and your own career, it will be your task not only to help the dancer in you, but also to dig inside and nurture, support and value the person in you who dances.

Procedure

All of the information in this book is completely in your hands. It is yours to read, to think about and sometimes to write about, and then to discuss with your fellow dancers.

After you have dealt with the material to your satisfaction, if you so choose, you can arrange for a senior artist to meet with you and your fellow students to discuss in greater detail issues that need clarification.

Before your meetings you can decide if you want to meet in one large group or in several smaller groups. You might want to appoint one person to co-ordinate the proceedings as group leader and one to take the few notes that will be necessary from time to time.

Here are a few things to think about:

❑ Participation is not compulsory. You can do all or part of what is suggested. Sometimes listening will be enough.

❑ There is some autobiographical writing suggested. As you know, writing about something often results in thoughts emerging that would remain under cover otherwise, so try at least to make a start. You may find yourself satisfied with only a few words when doing some personal exploration, or you may find yourself writing volumes. Whatever you come up with is exactly right. If you feel the information is too personal to share, remember that there is no obligation to do so. The important thing is for you to get the benefit of the process.

❏ Your words are neither good nor bad but simply an honest-as-you-can-be reflection of where you've been, where you are and where you hope to go.

❏ If you decide initially only to listen, leave yourself open to the idea that hearing others speak may give you the desire to do likewise.

❏ You very likely need each others' support. Sharing and giving feedback are important. If it feels more comfortable, share with only one person you trust.

❏ Take some risks.

❏ Remember, this book is not meant to be a lecture telling you what to do. It is meant to give you background information from which you can make your own discoveries and choices. A group of people with similar experiences and goals can truly support one another and share with one another in a most effective way.

Acknowledgments

There are many people I want to thank.

First of all, there is Joysanne Sidimus, whose energy, intellect and generosity of spirit are constantly supporting our dance community.

I am grateful to Marian Horosko and Judith R.F. Kupersmith, MD, authors of *The Dancer's Survival Manual*, and Daniel Nagrin, author of *How to Dance Forever.* Their books offered me much useful information.

Finally, I must thank all the people I talked with, particularly the students, who were so generous, open and courageous in expressing their deepest concerns.

about the author

Kenny Pearl began studying dance in Toronto when he was 19, with David Earle and Patricia Beatty and at The National Ballet School. He graduated from the University of Toronto with a BA in English at the same time as his obsession with dance was hitting him. He went to New York to take a few classes and stayed for 13 years. He danced with the Martha Graham Dance Company and around the world with the Alvin Ailey American Dance Theater. He also performed over the years independently with a dozen other companies. He has taught in New York at the schools of the Graham and Ailey companies and at the High School of Performing Arts and in Toronto at the School of the Toronto Dance Theatre. He has been a guest teacher in Vancouver, Montreal, Mexico City and throughout the United States. He studied acting and wrote and performed comedy cabaret in New York for several years before coming back to Toronto in 1981. After a season performing at the Stratford Festival, he was artistic director of Toronto Dance Theatre from 1983 to 1987. Since then he has begun a successful business importing silver jewellery from South-East Asia, and most recently served as the director of the School of the Toronto Dance Theatre.

CHAPTER

1

Part 1

valuing dance and the dancer

Here are two stories:
- A man I know was a major international dance figure in the '50s and '60s. He performed with one of the great New York companies, travelling around the world and earning the praise of audiences, critics and his fellow artists. He has taught and lectured at colleges throughout the United States and, thanks to a great intellectual curiosity that resulted in constant research, he is able to speak wisely on a wide range of topics. Yet his mother and father would not take his career seriously. Whenever he visited home, his parents constantly bragged about his sister, a school teacher. But the man's work was not discussed, because his parents did not consider dance to be a respectable profession.

- A wonderful Canadian dancer, 32 years old, is a member of an excellent company. She has a boyfriend who is a doctor. The dancer has actually trained longer and at least as intensively as the doctor, reaching a degree of excellence that at least equals his. The doctor helps people, many of whom would rather not see him but cannot do without the expertise he offers. The dancer brings joy and inspiration — both are healing qualities — to the people who eagerly buy tickets to see her perform. The doctor earns a very good living, while the dancer lives close to the poverty line. It is easy for her to see how and why society values him. Despite her friend's support, she says she often hears a little voice in the back of her head telling her that she is somehow of less value than he is.

Both stories reveal a lack of professional pride —
one for dance on the part of someone outside the profession, the other for the profession on the part of a dancer
herself.

Many people still hold such attitudes toward dance
and dancers, despite the art form's new-found popularity.
These limitations affect the lives of dancers and the life of
dance itself.

For example, very few top European universities
teach dance, though they often teach the other arts. We're
doing better here in North America, although very few
major Canadian universities or U.S. Ivy League colleges
teach dance except as a minor diversion. Ask a dancer
who takes part in a lot of lecture-demonstrations how
many times he or she has been asked, "Do you make
money doing this?"

It seems strange to us, so deeply involved in this
demanding and challenging profession, that there actually
are people out there who do not see dance as a serious,
respectable profession. Their point of view in part reflects
perceptions conjured up by the media, imposed by traditional beliefs and, perhaps, infused into the collective
unconscious by the events of the history of dance itself.

Unlike the plays and visual art work of earlier times,
which could be passed on because they could be
recorded, dance's past has come to us in two ways. The
first is directly, through observation of the dances of
peoples whose ancient cultural traditions have managed to
survive to the present. These peoples include certain tribes
in Africa and North America and the people of the island
of Bali in Indonesia. The forms and spirit of these dances
have influenced many 20th-century choreographers,
including Martha Graham and the Canadian artist Jean-
Pierre Perrault. When we have the opportunity to watch
these dances, what we may feel most strongly is that there

is in their rhythms an energy and spirit, an instinctual and passionate connection to the cycles of life and the rhythms of nature. Dance is performed as a way of connecting the people to their deities, of helping them control the forces of nature, and of bringing wholeness to a person, to a community or to the planet. Dancers are nurtured and respected. The life of the community may depend on their powers.

The second way dance's past comes to us is indirectly, through the descriptions in words and pictures of the people who populate our written history. What follows is a brief and simplified history of this development of western dance up to the early 1900s and from the point of view of professional pride:

To start on a bright note, it is encouraging to know that the people who gave us democracy, the discus thrower, *Oedipus Rex* and the Parthenon also liked to dance.

In ancient Greece, dance was an integral part of life. The Greeks, statesmen and military generals included, danced in public on special occasions. People were encouraged to dance to express the sorrows of tragic events and the joys of celebration, as well as the visions of playwrights. Dance was regularly a part of theatrical productions, along with words and music. From Euripides's last play, *The Bacchants,* come these words:

Cadmus, the old king of Thebes: Where do we dance? Where do we plant our feet and toss our old, grey heads? ... I shall never weary, night or day, beating the earth with the thyrsus. In my happiness I have forgotten how old I am.

Tiresius, a blind prophet: Then you feel as I do. I, too, feel young again. I, too, shall attempt the dance.

Cadmus: Shall we be the only ones in the city to dance for Bacchus?

Tiresius: We alone are right. The others are wrong. *

---

* *The Bacchants* from *Euripides: The Plays*, Bantam Books, June 1979

Perhaps one reason why dance was so naturally accepted by the ancient Greeks was that the human body was respected and enjoyed, not inhibited and feared. The Greeks had a very humane attitude toward the body and its possibilities. They created statues that reflected an ideal beauty that was meant to inspire nobility of thought and action and placed them in public places. They not only said that it was good to have a body, but that it was good to have a beautiful and expressive body. Although this statement may seem very straightforward to most of you so involved with creative expression through physicality, it was actually a revolutionary belief, one that has not often been held, before or since.

The results of the ancient Greeks accepting physicality and sensuality as part of the natural order were an exploration of possibilities that included the Olympics and the idea of having a sensual life without guilt, including romantic relationships, and dance.*

In all their expressions of the physical, as well as in every other aspect of their lives, the Greeks' ideal was balance, or sophrosyne, which meant moderation. They achieved balance by accepting the existence of opposites, both rational and ecstatic. There were times for "letting go" and times for "being civilised." These complementary opposites were both seen as essential to life and were embodied by Dionysus, the god of wine and of an orgiastic religion celebrating the power and fertility of nature, and Apollo, the god of the sun, prophecy, music, medicine and poetry. Without balance, which led to moderation, life was difficult. With it, life moved forward in positive ways.

---

* Many Greek deities were female. Women danced in the Dionysian rites and were often the subjects of sculptures and paintings. Still, men dominated in the worlds of politics, the arts and sports.

Sadly, the Greeks' sense of balance was lost when power shifted to Rome. With the establishment of the Roman Empire in 27 BC, balance disappeared — and our bodies and dance have been getting very mixed reviews ever since.

Initially, the people's participation in the arts remained unchanged. However, with the shift from a democracy to an empire, appreciation for the arts took the place of creating art. Once taught to all male Roman youths, dance was now left to slaves and imported Greeks. Dance, which had helped people find an emotional balance by participating as performers or audience, now became pure entertainment. The times produced wonderful pantomimes, but as the Empire began its decline, cruel gladiator games and other degrading spectacles in which dance was used only as filler became predominant.

When the Church came to Rome, the two symbols of the extremes of Apollo and Dionysus stood facing each other in complete opposition, each without a balancing energy to give real dignity to human life.

Every society has rituals and rules that encourage what it values and inhibit what it fears. The traditional Judaeo-Christian God as Our Father watched His flock, making sure the sensual experiences of the body were kept to a minimum and that guilt, if and when physical pleasure was experienced for its own sake, was encouraged to the maximum. Of course, there were reasons of survival that seemed to necessitate this point of view, and there were some dreadful situations that clearly warranted a bolt of lightning or two. Still, with sex being condoned only for reproduction, the message was "don't enjoy your body." Not only that, another message said: "Hide your body so you will not encourage sensual thoughts in others." Which brings us to dance. Too much enjoyment of the body — even the sight of it— was taboo, and acceptable physical expression was limited to battles and carefully prescribed ceremonies and rituals.

So with the ascendency of the Church, dance became an unacceptable form of human behaviour. A violent backlash followed, and the extreme decadence of the doomed Roman Empire was replaced by the opposite extreme of the Church. The reaction was so strong that, outside of the rare Medieval spectacle, there was to be no professional dance on any respectable European stage for around a thousand years.

The English poet Geoffrey Chaucer wrote *The Canterbury Tales*, Gregorian chants were sung, and the glorious cathedrals of Chartres, Rheims and St. Denis were built. However, the evolution of dance stopped. It is impossible to imagine what was lost in terms of the development of our art form as other arts continued to develop.

With the infusion of the values of the Renaissance in the 14th century, dance experienced a rebirth. Dance masters appeared who gradually evolved a technique as they taught the nobles dances to show off their wealth and position. These dances often were based on myths to show off the education of their students. Although great strides forward were achieved, this work clearly did not embrace the weighty themes and deep feelings of the work of the great Renaissance painters and sculptors. The art of dance during the two centuries of the Renaissance was regarded mainly as spectacle and entertainment.

This path led to the great achievements in the arts of Louis XIV, the French king who in 1669 formed the Royal Academy of Music and Dance (L'Opéra), which included the first professional dance company. The women of that company, encouraged by a male-dominated management (and society), did not help give dance a serious reputation as they flirted with the aristocracy and bourgeoisie during performance. However, with the support of royalty and a formal institution to give it credibility, dance gained the momentum to keep developing until it finally emerged in the 1830s and '40s as a highly respected art form.

During this period, ballet dancers were treated as artists, with the expressive dancing of the Romantic ballerinas Marie Taglioni and Carlotta Grisi in *La Sylphide* and *Giselle* leading the way. These ballets did not convey the real-life passions of William Shakespeare's *Hamlet* or *King Lear*, plays being seen at the time. But they impressed the public (and have stayed with us, perhaps) because, for one reason, underneath their supernatural stories they presented life truths — in *La Sylphide*, that you can kill love by trapping it; in *Giselle*, that love is stronger than death. For another, these dances idealized women, presenting them on the saint end of the spectrum, the other end of which was the flirtatious dancer of the court of Louis XIV and of the Paris Opéra of the late 1800s. Despite the artistry of this period, women (and men) weren't perceived as ordinary humans, only as such idealized beings as sylphs and princes.

Sadly, this period of great artistry came to an end with the repressed and heavily clothed moral climate of the Victorian period. During the 1870s and '80s, the ballet became a place for men to see scantily-clad women. Even male roles such as Franz in *Coppélia* were performed by women as an excuse to show women's legs more revealingly. Men were used to partner but seldom as virtuoso soloists.

Fortunately, during this time the Russians preserved the great dances and dancers. But at the Paris Opéra, the rehearsal hall, Le Foyer de la Danse, served as a place for ballerinas to meet the wealthy subscribers who were allowed free access. During this time the words female dancer became synonymous with mistress. When the revolutionary American dancer Isadora Duncan first visited the ballet, what she probably saw was a girly show, with corseted ballerinas making eyes at men in the audience, performing hard, mechanical moves with none of the expressive qualities associated with the earlier Romantic period. No wonder she, and others following closely after her, reacted so violently, feeling the need to return to the roots of dance and re-discover its expressiveness, passion and spontaneity.

Since the turn of the century, dance has made up for lost time, as its artists constantly and vigorously explore the possibilities of imagination, emotion and craft. And perhaps because of the various changes in behaviour and thinking during the past three decades — which we associate with the sexual revolution, the growth of feminism and the fitness craze — people have grown more accepting of and also more curious about the possibilities of their physicality.

The Hollywood film industry has responded to this new devotion to physicality by creating movies on the subject that can be successfully marketed to its largest audience — youth. In other words, films about dance are being produced that celebrate youth in facile ways, not by showing the growth of artists and their real-life struggles. In one film, high school students study dance along with math and history and in a semester or two are out-dancing members of the Alvin Ailey American Dance Theater. In another, a shy teenager struggles to learn dirty dancing, for a couple of weeks, then not only gives a great performance but falls in love at the same time.

In the past decade we've had flash dancing, break dancing and dirty dancing and the fads continue. As dancers, we can all have fun at some of these movies, using our experience to put them in proper light. However, for the general public, the blood, sweat and tears that go into and come out of a dancer's life are seriously trivialised.

Perhaps there is a silver lining inside the dark cloud of misinformation that current dance films are communicating to the public. Perhaps one of the results of all the recent social upheaval, the consciousness raising and even of the facile films about dance is that a breakthrough has taken place. Once again — and it took a long time — more and more people are saying, as the ancient Greeks did, that it is not only all right to have a body, it's all right to have a beautiful and expressive body. This belief represents a giant shift in a long-held point of view. In part because of this new belief, dance is enjoying its greatest popularity ever.

On the other hand, in March 1989 the Toronto Star ran a page 1 article whose headline reported: "... twirling tutu was just too, too titillating." Nova Scotia's telephone company, Maritime Tel, had produced a new telephone book whose cover featured a painting of a pair of figure skaters. The woman's legs, as in performance, were bare. Maritime Tel's vice-president explained: "There's a suggestion it could be offensive." So 100,000 covers were destroyed — and a lot of money was spent on new covers! Can dance flourish in a society where such puritanical sensibilities still exist? Will people who think like that be eager to buy tickets to watch you dance? These are good questions to consider.

We react to the profession and are reacted to by others more than ever in ways that show respect for the greatness of our art and the process of a dancer's life. The lingering messages of a troubled history, a false impression of dance created in Hollywood, and the ever-present rules of a society that bans an ice skaters' legs from the cover of a phone book are some of the things that still keep too many out there, including my American friend's parents, from getting to know us and being enriched by all we have to offer.

Many people put aside, or are forced to give up, their dreams to make money and find obvious security. The greatest value must be put on the choice made by people who risk everything to do that for which they have a passion. A lot of people out there gave up their dreams a long time ago. They will deeply respect, envy or not even care about your brave choices. They probably will find something awakened in themselves if they allow themselves to open up to the physical and emotional possibilities of your dream.

In groups

We have looked briefly at how society's point of view concerning dance and dancers is, and has been, affected in various ways. If you can relate in any way to the American dancer who has relations who fail to take dance and the dancer seriously, or if you are like the Canadian dancer who fails to value a life in dance as highly as a life in a more obviously valuable profession, it may be good now to ask some questions about what a life in dance has to offer you and what you and dance have to offer society. Your observations and insights can give you a feeling of confidence in your profession. Firm beliefs in what you are doing may help keep your spirits up and your path clear if and when you encounter obstacles either from within or from without.

1. A good starting point may be to discuss some of the ideas presented in the stories of the two dancers. Take the time to raise your own questions after looking at them.

2. Choose one or any number of these questions that concern you:

— How are the perceptions of the people you are close to affected by the recent Hollywood dance films, by religious beliefs, or by "uptight" attitudes about the expressive possibilities of the human body?

— How does people's recognition of Apollonian (being civilised) and Dionysian (letting go) energies affect their feelings about dance and dancers?

— When you tell people you're studying to become a dancer, how do they react? Do women's reactions differ from men's? Do people seem to know what to say to you? Do you feel you're being taken as seriously as someone who may be studying to become a lawyer?

3. The role of the artist in society has been a topic of concern lately, as various organizations make their pitches for funding, hoping to show enough positive inter-connection to receive financial support. For the artist, exploring the relationship of his/her profession to the world he/she lives in can create a more holistic vision of that world, in which a dancer often feels quite isolated. So, to begin with:

— What are the roles of the artist in society today?

— How do the performing arts affect society — culturally, socially, economically, politically and ideologically?

— What does dance have to offer its audience? How can it affect its audience?

— What do you, as a dancer, have to share with those with whom you make contact, on stage or off?

— What does dance have to give to you that differentiates it from most other professions?

— In what ways does your path make you unique?

— What are an artist's responsibilities?

4. Dancers often fear that because they are trained specifically to be dancers, they are poorly prepared to do anything else. The truth, more likely, is that if you have become a dancer, you have developed along the way skills to pursue many interests.

As a dancer you are developing, without thinking about it, transferable skills that will enable you to explore, thoroughly and quickly, new interests for which you have an aptitude. Knowing that you are growing in dance in a very full way can add to your sense of pride, and also give you an extra measure of confidence and security. It is doubtful that many professions prepare an individual in such a variety of ways, so the idea of transferable skills is one worth researching.

Dr. Scot McFadden and Dr. David Tucker are two of the Dancer Transition Centre's Toronto resource professionals in the field of career counselling. Based on their experience with dancers, they recently compiled a list of transferable skills most dancers have acquired. These include "a desire to refine and improve one's existing skills" and "the ability to follow direction and coaching of superiors."

— Take some time now to make your own list of transferable skills. Try to come up with at least a dozen. Have someone write them down.

In a profession with so many ups and downs, with so many misconceptions directed toward it, it is helpful to have as realistic a sense of pride in what you are doing as possible. Your responses to the preceding questions and tasks can expand your beliefs about dance in ways that will be of value to you.

Part 2

valuing the you who dances

T hinking about how dancers feel about themselves probably will project into how and what they communicate to an audience, as well as to fellow dancers, choreographers and teachers. How they feel about themselves will also have a lot to do with how personally fulfilled they are with their own accomplishments.

In a profession that requires so much discipline, dancers must necessarily be critical of their own work and be able to take criticism from others. Dealing with criticism from the outside is part of the process of a dancer's life. In the constant struggle to keep improving, self-criticism is also necessary. It can be helpful, but if it is based on an unrealistic sense of self, as too often is the case, self-criticism can be defeating.

Many dancers are their own *worst* critics. If you are a "worst critic," there may be a moment in class when you look at all the other dancers (who may be looking back at you for the same reason) and begin a ritual of comparisons in which you inevitably decide that someone is better than you. Or your self-criticism may involve only a dissatisfied you and the mirror. The "too's" often lead the way — I am too tall or too short, too heavy or too thin, too dramatic or too lyrical. "Someone always does the variation better than me" or "if I am the best, it's just not good enough." In other words, if you do not take pride in your physicality and are looking for a way to put yourself down, you'll find it. Not feeling good about yourself can distort reality, making a helpful criticism hurt and making a compliment given to someone else a cause for jealousy and anger.

Of course, intelligent self-criticism is important and some dancers, often the most outstanding, are their own *best* critics. Best critics accept differences because they have a sense of pride in their own individuality. Best critics have setbacks, but also have an ability to move forward because they weigh everything said to them, good and bad, use what is helpful and let go of the rest. They are happy to see others doing well because they believe there is enough good out there for everyone who works hard and has his or her own measure of talent.

If we put a totally life-enhancing sense of self at one end of the self-esteem spectrum, and a completely destructive sense of self at the other, we all will find ourselves somewhere in between.

Here are two lists for you to examine. They are not meant to define you, but to give you a point of departure.

A) Dancers With Healthy Self-Esteem	**B) Dancers With Unhealthy Self-Esteem**
Have realistic goals and believe in the possibility of their fulfillment.	Don't believe attainment of their goals is likely.
Enjoy life. When things don't work out, don't feel sorry for themselves for long, but take action to make changes. They are in control	Feel life is a struggle. Feel self-pity. Feel out of control.
Are happy to see others do well.	Are threatened by others doing well.

Accept a mistake as a mistake, learn from it and move on. Appreciate fair criticism.	Believe a mistake is an indication of how bad they really are. Feel a sense of panic when they are criticized.
Do not like to gossip.	Gossip a lot. Need to feel good about saying negative things about others.
Are helpful to others as well as to themselves.	Are interested mainly in helping themselves.
Have patience, tolerance and an honest balance of pride and humility.	Are impatient, intolerant and are either too humble or too arrogant.
Take pride in their physicality.	Never like how they look.
Take pride in their accomplishments.	Never feel what they have done is good enough.
Compete in a healthy way, enjoying the challenge others offer. Compete with themselves, challenging their own standards.	Compete to prove they're better than someone else. Competition scares them because they don't believe they're very good at what they do.

Have a lifestyle that is life enhancing.	Have a lifestyle that has destructive elements.
Attract and keep friends who are supportive.	Establish friendships in which they are used.
May get nervous but are energized by people watching.	Are made painfully nervous by being watched.
Show feelings in appropriate ways.	Are emotionally blocked. Have highly exaggerated reactions.

Having read through the lists, you may want to add some other characteristics that you feel apply.

If all the points in List B applied to you, you'd probably be in prison by now and not in a dance studio. If you embraced List A wholeheartedly, you'd be a saint in heaven. The truth, more likely, is that we all have some of these characteristics some of the time. Your own balance of these qualities may say a lot about your general state of happiness and your ability to work productively. Reading through the lists, you probably mentally checked off descriptions you felt related to you. So now let's take this bit of self-examination a step further.

On your own

A self portrait

From your knowledge of yourself, compose a self-portrait from the point of view of self esteem. Include in your description:
— How you see yourself—physically, emotionally and any other way
— How you think others see you
— How you see others in class, both teachers and classmates
— How you feel your behaviour affects others
— How the behaviour of others affects you
— Is your attitude toward yourself and your perceived attitude of others holding you back or moving you forward?

Before writing, consider this possibility:
You may have become so used to your own behaviour and feelings that qualities that hold you back or that move you forward may be taken for granted, going unnoticed.
Remember, you may find yourself stuck with a few words or you may write volumes. If you spend some time exploring and writing, you probably will make some interesting and important discoveries. If you feel the information is too personal to share, remember that there is no obligation to do this for anyone but yourself. This self-esteem self portrait is not good or bad, positive or negative. It's just meant to be an as-honest-as-you-can-be picture of where you are inside yourself at this point in your life.

In groups

Remember that there are a number of ways in which you can participate when you are together in your groups. You can participate by listening, by commenting and being supportive and by sharing your portrait. Do what is comfortable. The chances are that once you get involved, hearing what others have written and sensing the support being offered, you will feel safer in sharing your own experiences.

— If you read your portrait and get feedback, do the comments indicate that you are being too hard on yourself?

— Do you see yourself differently than others see you?

— Have you missed qualities completely?

— How does all this make you feel?

— Do others share similar traits and does sharing your experiences and feelings make you feel more accepting of yourself?

Rewrite your self-portrait from time to time, so you can see how as you accumulate experience, you change. Making note of changes for the better can be very encouraging.

Our life-enhancing qualities make us feel good as they earn us praise, but mainly because they help our lives move forward in positive ways. It is important to appreciate yourself and one another for these qualities. Knowing that you have always done your best will create a personal support system that will help you stay on top when you encounter setbacks.

The qualities that give us cause for concern are the ones that hold us back. Recognizing them as you have begun to do is a good first step in changing them.

Too often, however, despite our greatest efforts to do otherwise, we find ourselves clinging to those very qualities that are doing us no good at all. Obviously, we don't intellectually choose to be angry or jealous or to be painfully shy. There just seems to be a little voice in the back of our heads that keeps giving us unhelpful messages. These messages — like "I'm not good enough" or "I don't deserve all this" — can cause us to make choices that hurt. Sometimes it seems as if we are the recipient of these negative messages, but the messages themselves are something we did not choose.

From birth, through the way our parents' eyes meet ours, the quality of their touch, the feeling in their voices, we all get messages about our bodies. These messages give us our first, and most say our strongest, impressions about what is good about our bodies and what is bad, what behaviour is acceptable and what is off limits, what we can freely do and what must be hidden.

The feelings caused by rivalries with our siblings can stay with us as adults, causing unwelcome feelings of jealousy and envy.

Our parents have reactions to our personal acts of independence and to our creative impulses. Sometimes they take great joy in the surprises we offer. Sometimes they feel threatened, because our actions don't fit into their game-plan for us.

Early experiences with perfectionist teachers and parents may also leave lasting impressions.

The media is constantly putting in front of us a very specific idea of what is beautiful, particularly concerning women.

We may grow up with predominantly positive feelings about ourselves. On the other hand, we may find ourselves believing — without thinking twice about it — that our bodies are not as beautiful as they are, that too many of our feelings and longings are not safe to express, and that no matter what we do, we will never be quite good enough or deserving enough.*

* Hundreds of books have been written about the messages given to vulnerable children and their lasting effects; and dozens of points of view have been put forward. If the subject interests you, head for a good bookstore to sort through the variety of full-bodied discussions available.

With all the gifts of your talent and training, and with your own personal mix of messages, you are choosing a profession in which criticism is very often present. From the responses of teachers and choreographers through auditions and casting choices to the reactions of audiences to the reviews of critics, someone is usually reacting to you. They may be reacting with words, the quality of their look, or by not noticing you at all.

It is believed that movement never lies and that your body reflects your truth. If you take pride in your physicality, believe in your performance as a gift to share and are energized by all the eyes watching you, you probably will grow in achievement and fulfillment, using what sensible criticism you need to help you in that direction.

Believing that you, on stage performing, are a gift to share has nothing to do with how conventionally beautiful you are. It's a question of such things as underlying personality and life-enhancing beliefs. Some bodies with the most unlikely shapes take the stage and, with their own magic, which might include qualities of intelligence, sensitivity and imagination, deeply move us. Have you ever seen someone you've admired on stage walk into a studio and been shocked because they do not look nearly as beautiful, charismatic and powerful as you had perceived from the audience? Have you ever seen someone who is gorgeous in class appear on stage and put you to sleep?

Dancers who do not take enough pride in their physical being, or who feel they are not good enough or don't deserve to be successful are often made uncomfortable by all those watching eyes. No matter how physically beautiful, talented or even passionate they are, many dancers tend to find performance difficult, sometimes even traumatic. A general audience may pick up their discomfort. A seasoned dance observer will usually notice it right away. Not really enjoying oneself can make the biggest smile seem false. Emotional pain can transform a beautiful physical line into something tense and unwatchable. *"I work hard and I dance well, but there are some things about myself I don't like. Sometimes I get self-conscious because I think the audience is noticing."*

Other fine dancers find performance to be a high, with their difficulty coming after: *"I love performing. My problem starts when I go back to my room and start going through my performance. I get out of control agonizing over every little thing that was okay before but now is just not good enough. My happiness with myself disappears."*

Criticism, from inside or outside, will cause an exaggerated reaction when it gives weight to the already limiting beliefs that you may hold about yourself.

Being human, it is easy to accept the limitations imposed on us. They can cause us to feel and behave in ways that can be frightening and confusing. *"Right now I'm probably more confused than I have ever been.... I'm dealing with so many different emotions, feelings and doubts. It gets hard to distinguish what is and isn't right for me. I suppose I'll find out what I want sooner or later."*

In the introduction, "good" confusion was discussed as being a part of a natural process of growth. Now it is important to remember that if you are feeling confused, it is possible to gain an understanding of the ways of feeling, seeing and believing that are holding you back, and to change them.

You probably will choose to change them if your love of dance, your enjoyment of dancing and your need to do it are sincere and strong.

You will be able to change because you have an abundance of emotional, intellectual and physical resources inside you.

You will be able to change if you gain the self-knowledge that allows you to evaluate your situation.

You will be able to change if you have the right kind of support to deal with what is distressing you. Being able to learn to express your feelings in the appropriate setting helps.

It is not unnatural to be depressed, dissatisfied or anxious from time to time. Sometimes such practical techniques as positive thinking, creative visualization and meditation can deal with reversing a temporary setback. Sometimes the attention and support of a caring friend or teacher can help. Many shy, awkward students have gone on to do amazing things because a teacher believed in them and created a loving atmosphere they could trust and in which they could grow. In most cases, knowing the cause of your distress and doing some self-examination and/or talking to an appropriate friend can help you deal with what you are feeling. Sometimes, just having an awareness of the situation you are in, its cause and effect, is enough to turn it around. That is one reason spending some time looking back into your own past can be helpful.

Sometimes, however, the stress has a deeply rooted cause. The resulting distress may not be temporary but may persist no matter how hard you try to change it. If you have troubles that have been with you, not necessarily consistently but over a period of months or even years, it probably is time to do some much deeper exploring of yourself.

Be selective about who you talk with about these problems. Nothing is more damaging than well-meaning amateur therapists. If you feel therapy or counselling is necessary, consult the Dancer Transition Centre in Toronto for the name of an appropriate organization in your area to give you information, or the head of your school for the names of counsellors with the right kind of experience and knowledge.

It is important to remember that it is not unusual to go through discouraging times. The world of dance can be hard enough — not offering financial security, taking up so much of our time that social interaction with others outside dance is limited, very often involving some degree of physical pain. On top of these stresses may be your own personal troubles.

Dance has much to offer, so much to enjoy. It is important for your sense of achievement and fulfillment to have the means to clear away what is getting in your way and become your own best critic, having strong feelings of your own self-worth.

Examining your past and how it affects your present is one way of gaining a deeper understanding of yourself and gaining more control to make the best choices for yourself regarding personal distress. If you love dance, your passion for it and need to do it probably will carry you for a time through just about any obstacle, no matter how painful.

It will certainly make your life in dance more long lasting, creative, enjoyable and fulfilling if you don't just bash through the obstacles but find a greater sense of personal wholeness by actually dealing intelligently with them.

On your own

You have looked at how you are relating to yourself and to others and at how the quality of those relationships makes you feel. Now try some personal history exploration. Explore some of the messages you've gotten in the past that may be causing you to relate in these ways.

In groups

Share some of your cause-and-effect discoveries. How do you deal with your own short-term setbacks? You may have something helpful to share.

CHAPTER
2

Part 1

the "why"
of your involvement with dance

I t will be interesting, possibly even enlightening, for you to look at the big question of *why* you started to dance. Your thoughts on this subject will go a long way toward giving you an increased understanding of your relationship to dance, and of why that relationship makes you feel and act the way you do.

Dance may become a necessary obsession for many reasons, with deeper layers of understanding rising to the surface as one gains in experience. Since there usually is more than meets the eye in determining reasons for a choice as all-encompassing as being a dancer, perhaps no two people's motivations are exactly the same. Still, conversations with many dancers show that there seem to be a number of similar points of entry.

Basically, participants fall into two broad divisions — those who begin dance as children or in their early teens, and those who start as young adults.

Most within the western tradition of ballet and modern dance who are involved in dance early in life usually begin their training in ballet.* They arrive in class, possibly starry eyed, possibly confused. Here's how some who began with ballet classes remember starting:

---

* A growing number of what can loosely be called creative dance classes are being offered to very young children, usually in connection with modern dance schools. It will be interesting to see how these classes affect the people involved in making career choices later in life.

"I had so much energy, my parents didn't know what to do with me. So I ended up in Miss Wilke's School of Ballet, Tap and Baton Twirling three nights a week."

"My mom wanted to dance but never had the chance, so she got me all excited about doing it. Sometimes I still can't tell if I'm doing it for myself or for her."

"I saw The Nutcracker when I was 7 and begged my mom to let me take class."

"Life at home was a mess. My parents enrolled me in a full-time school so I wouldn't have to watch their marriage fall apart. It was the best thing they ever did for me."

"I came from a very poor family. I applied for a scholarship to do this because, as the girl sings in A Chorus Line, 'everything was beautiful at the ballet.'"

"I can never remember a time when I did not want to dance."

Most who start dance later in life have been raised in basically "traditional" family settings and, even if some participation in the arts has been encouraged, a life in dance is not the direction they are encouraged to take.

Still, after realizing there are likely to be long hours, physical pain, compromises in their social lives because of touring and little money, many people are pulled into dance and stay involved for many years. Their passion for it and need to perform, their experience of its immediate pleasures and the growth the work encourages, as well as their dreams of achievement are greater than the effects of all the stress.

If you started to dance in your late teens or 20s, chances are you began on your own and had no choice but to get involved and stay involved once you knew a certain kind of dance existed.

"I saw a revival of the musical West Side Story when I was in my first year of law in New York. I knew, then, in spite of how impossible it seemed, that I would dance."

For some, dance offers a more challenging continuation of early interests.

"I was always involved in athletics, particularly diving, because I liked the challenge of complex co-ordinations. Dance seemed to offer the ultimate challenge."

Many people decided on a life in dance because it offered them something they felt (perhaps unconsciously at the time) was missing in themselves. The world of dance gave them a place to express in ways that had been inhibited. Certainly dance, with its energy and sensuality, physical expressiveness and virtuosity, passion and make-believe, as well as the promise of applause (approval, love) has much to offer. Through dance, a dancer can find a degree of balance.

"When I was little, I was taught to be seen and not heard, to always be polite. I remember always reading and never playing. I withdrew a lot. It even surprised me when I got this incredible desire to dance, but now I realize that I saw dance as a way to feel and be physical and be appreciated for it."

"I felt ordinary and thought dance could make me extraordinary."

It often seems to dancers as if they didn't choose dance, but that dance chose them. In fact, if there was a time when you sat down and tried to decide if you wanted to dance or do something else, you probably wouldn't be reading this now. A carpenter who once was a dance student said:

> *"The day I thought to myself, 'I don't know whether I should stay in dance or get involved with woodworking full time,' was the day I knew I would soon be leaving dance."*

Most dancers, no matter how or why they began, seem to love dancing very much. However, some dancers — as well as other performers of all kinds — believe that life is required to be a struggle. They tend to enjoy, even to live for, the struggle to dance more than the dancing itself.

There are many reasons for this. One might be that the need to struggle is encouraged by some traditional western religions, which teach that to accomplish anything good, one must suffer. One need not be a "religious" person to be affected by this point of view.

Also, some people just love to complain, and thrive on getting sympathy. The world of dance, with all its hardships, provides them with a perfect environment in which to indulge themselves.

Some are attracted to the hard life of dance because they want to show the world how tough they are. They want everyone to see that they are better and stronger because they can rise above all the stress, no matter how tired or in pain they may be. A martyr feels better and stronger than others and lets you know, gaining your attention and praise.

If this kind of exploration is of ongoing interest to you, you probably will find that as your involvement with dance grows and your experiences accumulate, your understanding of your pull into dance will deepen. You may also discover that as you go on, your reasons for staying in dance change.

"I was the fifth of seven children and didn't get much attention. Without realizing it, I danced to prove to the world that I was worth noticing. But the applause was never enough. I always felt second best. After some counselling, I started to understand why I felt and acted the way I did. Every day now, I seem to dance less because I feel I have to prove something and more because I really love, for myself, the challenges that dance offers."

On your own

1. And now for the first and inevitable question: Why did you start to dance? Keep this question floating around in the back of your mind for a few days and see what discoveries you make.

2. You began dancing for certain reasons. After all these years, are your reasons for staying involved different?
What has changed about you that makes your reasons for staying in dance different?

3. Can you make any connections between your reasons for starting dance and your sense of self-esteem?

In groups

1. Discuss your discoveries to the degree that you are comfortable.

2. Does hearing what others have to say give you fresh insights?

Part 2

developing depth and range as an artist

By the time dancers reach the point where they're ready to make the change to professional life, as you are now, most know what it means to be committed, dedicated and to have the ability to work as hard as possible to acquire a strong physical technique. Knowing what the companies you hope to join want and knowing how few spaces there will be in them puts pressure on each of you to focus strongly on the development of physical skills.

This drive to achieve an appropriately outstanding technique is both necessary and time consuming. But it may cause you to pay insufficient attention to other aspects of your work and of your life, aspects essential to the evolution of a fullness that reveals your uniqueness in ways increasingly satisfying to you, to choreographers and to audiences.

Acquiring a technique is a difficult and ongoing process, but if you are taught well and work hard enough and intelligently for long enough, you will acquire technique. You may have to change your goals based on how your technique develops, but if they are realistic, you probably will find a place.

However, being content with having obtained work and having appeared on stage to show off one possibility (physical virtuosity) of a multi-faceted art form is to be content with limitation. Unfortunately, it is easy to fall into the trap of limitation. Training can focus so much on one dimension because of the results required to get work. (I've even heard teachers say, "Work on technique now. Artistry will come later.") Being one-sided is unfair to everyone — to you, given your incredible resources of imagination and emotion; to your choreographers, who depend on you to express their visions; and to the people in the audience, who need not only to be impressed by your physical abilities but to be moved by your individuality as well.

Whether as a company member or as an independent artist, you probably will be working with a wide variety of choreographers throughout your career. They will expect you to respond to their directions not just with the power of your physical virtuosity but with a sense of your individuality and uniqueness. Most choreographers don't just look for a dancer, but for the person who dances.

This sense of oneself, this individuality, is a result of so many things, some of which a dancer does not consciously bring to dance but many of which can be deliberately developed. These attributes involve a balance in the way dancers develop dance skills and a balance in the way they develop life skills.

Dance skills involve not only the technical considerations emphasized in daily class. To give the most of themselves, dancers must also learn to explore other dimensions of dance so that their performance is not only a physical display but also a rich and unique coming together of their artistry with a composer's and a choreographer's vision.

Dancers must learn to express the emotional content of their movement; they must be musical in a way that is not rigid but enables them to dance with, or through, or against the music. They must learn to move in ways that can transform movement through shifting dynamics, revealing subtle qualities of the choreography. The dancer must also be able to break down qualities that may have been associated in training with masculine or feminine ways to move, and be able to move in many ways.

Obviously, the development of these skills goes on throughout your career. But the time to start thinking about them and developing them is now, while you have time to work slowly and carefully and while you have many classes each day.

Developing as a physical dancer must be your main priority, but hiding in dance, withdrawing into its physicality at the expense of developing other sides of yourself, can lead the way to a variety of problems, both artistic and personal.

To be a dancer, you need not only physical skills but very strong life skills. You must be able to get along with all the members of a company on a six-week tour, keep your morale high and your health and finances in order. You must be able to deal with all the surprises new theatres can hold for you, endless bland hotel rooms and separations from friends, family and lovers at home. Then there are the casting emergencies, the chronic pains and the disappointments of layoffs due to injury or lack of company funds. To survive, a dancer needs emotional strength and flexibility, staying power and, perhaps most of all, a good sense of humour.

The relative isolation required by such a demanding and time-consuming profession results in some dancers having no outside interests, few inner resources (including social skills) and a social circle that includes only dancers. The world of dance is overwhelming and can come to seem like everything. As great as it can be, it is only one of many possible worlds. When the disappointments and routines and aches and pains of that world close in on you, as they probably will from time to time, it is important to have other worlds to dive into for refreshment and rejuvenation. It is also important to be able to talk about other things besides dance if you are to extend your circle of friends beyond dancers.

Some performers do outstanding work on stage but do not enjoy the opportunities of travel, of making friends outside dance, of reading novels or newspapers, of going to art galleries, of experiencing performances other than dance or even of investigating the possibilities of helping themselves through emotional pain. For these performers, living their lives so narrowly often brings on great difficulties as their careers progress. They face the threat of loneliness, withdrawal, boredom and a short career, because when their dance world falls apart, their whole world falls apart.

Discovering and exploring outside interests, meeting and communicating with people outside of dance and working on dispelling the personal demons that hold you back can enrich your life as a dancer. These activities can help you find a life-enhancing balance of dance, social events and academic endeavours that can help keep you involved longer as a healthy and passionate participant. They will also give you more fullness and inspiration to bring to your work.

Passion in one area of your life usually will spill into other areas. Just reading a good book will not only help you fill in those empty hours on buses and in hotel rooms but may expand your outlook, enrich your emotional life and give you insights into the workings of other characters (which may help you develop a character of your own for the stage). Seeing an art exhibit in a small town or the sights of a major city may give you more energy for your evening performance than the few hours extra sleep other dancers choose instead.

And making new friends outside of dance — which isn't always easy — or talking even briefly to someone at a post-performance reception can introduce you to new worlds, helping to keep your own in perspective. Developing social skills can be difficult, particularly if you have grown up in the cloistered world of a full-time ballet school. In their book *The Dancer's Survival*

Manual, authors Marian Horosko and Dr. Judith R.F. Kupersmith quote Dr. Stanley E. Greben, the consulting psychiatrist for the Dancer Transition Centre in Toronto, on the subject of maturity:

"It is my belief that one can learn to achieve emotional intimacy at any age. It may not be the same, since the normal time for interaction was postponed, but it is not an end to the possibility. How do you learn? If you are not in too much trouble with yourself, you must get out and meet new people and take more chances. Of course, that's not easy. But that is the best way out — on your own.

"If you are in too much trouble with that prospect, the way to break down barriers is with the help of a good therapist. Good therapy is an emotional experience, one that is a trusting relationship and will permit you to let down some protective devices. It may not be that you do not know what to do or how to do it, but that the barriers against hurt are best let down in the company of someone who is safe and well-meaning."

We have so far briefly looked at developing depth and range as a performer in two ways, by diversification in your training and by expanding your point of view outside your training. Finally, let's take a brief look at what depths might be achieved once you make a choice to stop accepting your personal suffering, doubts and fears (if you have them) as inevitable and do something about them.

A lot of dancers are unhappy, but are addicted to their own struggles, no matter what it costs them. Some believe that losing the kind of uniqueness that is causing them unhappiness and making their lives a struggle will result in their losing their creative spark. Others say that a person may be drawn to the art form because of that uniqueness but that the true artist will only emerge despite it, and more and more so as their doubts and fears disappear. In *The Dancer's Survival Manual*, Horosko and

Kupersmith write:

"Distress can immobilize talent, inhibit growth emotionally and physically, cause unnecessary unhappiness and limit the career. A free, joyful, unlimited creativity evolved without fear, in confidence, and with calculated risks to the full potential of the individual artist is the goal."

For now remember that your ability to achieve happiness and success will ultimately depend on more than hard work and good work in the studio. Finding the balance you need — dealing with some trial and error and taking some risks — will be the effort that gives a direction, and a life, to your talent.

This balance will be different for each of you, but will include developing in dance and beyond dance in as full and rich a way as possible. This balance may mean changing activities or beliefs that get in the way of your own free and joyful creativity.

At home

We've talked in this section about outside interests and you may have such a full schedule that you don't feel you have the time or energy or money to do much else than see a film once in a while. Chances are that if you find something that really interests you, you will find the time and energy for it and, surprisingly, find yourself with more energy for your dance.

What interests do you have outside of dance that you are pursuing even in the smallest way — photography, painting, astronomy, cooking, sports? Can you list five?

Are there activities you think of pursuing but have not yet tried? Make a list of these, in order of their importance to you. Consider investigating the one on the top of your list.

In groups

1. Discuss the extent to which you are getting information about aspects of dance other than technique in your various classes. Are you getting direction as to musicality, phrasing and dynamics? No one teacher can do everything, but make sure overall that you are getting everything you need to add colours to your work. Find a time to talk with your principal or director if you feel anything is lacking in your dancing.

2. For those with little money to spend on anything other than subsistence, dozens of activities connected with the arts are available in most cities at a cost of $5 or less.

Make a list of as many of these activities as you can. You probably will come up with enough suggestions to keep each of you busy for a year.

It might be a good idea to type up your list and post it in your school so all the students can benefit from it.

3. Do you believe your personal turmoil contributes to your creativity?

CHAPTER

3

Part 1

dealing with misinformation
and getting helpful information

For most serious dance students, the goal of all the years of training is performing, either with a company or as an independent artist. Most of the information you have absorbed from that training helps take you to that place. The specific focus of the information given is likely to make you the kind of dancer your school values the most, perhaps preparing you to join the company connected to that school or a company with similar values.

By the time you have almost completed your full-time school program, you may find that your life in dance is not moving as you had planned. Your goals, perhaps conceived years ago and encouraged in your school's program, may now seem out of reach, or they may now be out of touch with your changed desires and new progress. The specific focus of your school may cause you confusion if it leaves you without the ability to determine how you relate to the bigger world of dance outside your school's door.

What follows are the words of students at different schools who have come to realizations concerning their goals. They express a reaction to what the students see as misinformation or a lack of information. The students were training either in schools connected with companies or in schools with a specific point of view, both physical and philosophical, that makes entry into some companies more likely and acceptable than others.

1. Through daily exposure to the company's style and technique, which you may be told are the best, through your teacher's philosophical connections with the company, whose values you may be encouraged to believe are the best, and through regular exposure to the dancers in the company, some of whom you may see as the best, you start to believe — if you didn't on the day you arrived — that this company is the one you should be striving to join and that no other company is as worthy of your consideration.

"When I first came, I watched the company every chance I got. It inspired me to think that my teachers taught those dancers. Now I'm glad when they're on tour because they remind me that I just turned out to be a different kind of dancer, which isn't seen to be quite as good around here. My dream is gone and nothing has replaced it because the school always made me feel that settling for anything less than their company was just second best. Even though in my head I know there are lots of good companies I'm good enough to work with, I feel like a failure."

"After this year is finished, I have to make a big decision. I need a lot of information so I can re-define my goals if necessary, but I'm not getting that here."

"I'm a ballet dancer who is good enough for the company, but deep inside I know I'd like to dance with one of the modern companies I've seen. We're so sold on this company and on ballet for so many years that I'm ashamed to say that I can't help but feel very guilty even thinking this way. I don't know if I can make the change." *

---

* She made the change.

2. You come to realize there are only a few, if any, openings for positions in "the" company each year and you aren't sure where all your training is leading you.

"We are here to learn, to prepare for our own future, but are made to feel like our whole time here is an audition for the company. You can tell right away who the chosen ones are. The rest of us have to believe and know we're right for other places. I feel very lost."

3. You start to realize that some of the beliefs you were encouraged to have are, in fact, not completely appropriate.

"They encourage us to believe that all we need to join their company, or any company, is what they offer us here. We do it for years and then start to notice that the ones who are making it into the company are almost always those who came here with a lot of training in other areas and have the kind of technique some of us can't get here."

"I believe the abilities of the school are endless, as they are in life. As idealistic as this all sounds, why do I question the reality?"

"I'm here to find myself and stretch myself to the limit. I ask for a lot, but I don't understand what I'm getting. Life is precious, therefore everything must become clear. I'm unsatisfied."

"They tell us how their dance will solve all our problems — physical and emotional. If that's true, why do I and so many of my friends here have so much confusion and doubt?"

The pressure on these students is obvious. With only a confused sense of themselves and where they're going, with once-cherished goals gone and no new ones to replace them, a student may feel isolated and disillusioned enough to stop making steady progress. If you feel that this is in some way your predicament, it may be time for you to come to terms with beliefs concerning yourself and your goals that are not working for you.

Like many "last-year" students, you may have few ideas about what's happening next and may be filled with confusion and doubt. If next year holds unknowns for you, you have two basic choices. The first is to be a passive agent, waiting for some coincidence, stroke of luck, accident or connection to guide you to the right place. The second is to take control, making yourself an active agent, shaping your own future to whatever degree is possible, helping yourself to be the cause of being in the right place at the right time. You can do many things to expand your point of view in this context.

Being actively involved probably will improve your effectiveness, make you feel better and give you a heightened sense of yourself. Transition from school to professional life will be smoothest if your own assessment of yourself is clear, and if the directions you choose are based not only on that assessment but also on a full knowledge of all the possibilities in dance that are available to you. Your self-directed actions can help you see how you can either realize your original dream or how, if your old goals are no longer possible or desirable, you can discover new and challenging opportunities.

On your own

1. Self-assessment

Remember that the dancer who not only does well but also survives well has a clear and objective idea of the quality of her/his talent. With this in mind, take the time now to evaluate your artistry and talent, temperament and values, with regard to finding possible directions for yourself. You probably have heard your principal's or teachers' evaluations of you. Now, with their words in mind, do it on your own. Give this task a lot of attention. Many dancers who have gone on to do great things were told in their school evaluations that they were not good enough (but for what?). The people doing the evaluating may have been looking at them through glasses of only one colour. Listen, share with those you respect, get what you can from the point of view of others. That is all very important. However, for your own good you must ultimately be the one to take responsibility and make the final assessment.

Begin your dance self-portrait by exploring yourself in four ways.

1. Make a list of your skills. For example, are you strongest performing dramatic work, or abstract movement, or improvisation?

2. Make a list of your interests. For example, what kind of dance do you like the most? Do you want to work within a company that travels a lot or stays home? Do you want only to dance, or to be in a company that will encourage you to choreograph as well?

3. What about your temperament? For example, do you feel more comfortable being in a small company or is it all right if you are part of a large chorus? Do you need to participate actively or is just doing what you're told all right?

4. What about your values? What is important to you? Truth, beauty, conformity, popularity, service, achievement, freedom, integrity, security, status? Some sound like values you should have, while others seem selfish, but nobody's perfect. Be honest.

This assessment need be only for you. You will get clearer about the kind of company you are willing and able to work with when you clarify what it is you want to express and are able to express.

2. Goals

As part of the process leading to your exploration of goals, start by looking at the goals you began with, the ones you still have, the ones that now seem out of reach and your new goals. First, think about the comments of the dance students cited above.
— Do you relate to any of the things said?
— Are there other issues for you concerning information given and information not given that have confused you concerning your progress and your goals?
— Are your goals the same as when you first came to this school?
— If they've changed, why?
— What are your goals?
— If you don't have any goals, why not?
— Are your expectations realistic, based on your personal assessment?
— Are they realistic given the competition for the few places available?
— If old goals no longer seem realistic, are you sure you've given them up for the right reasons?

Some dancers who have the appropriate talent are very hard on themselves, believing they aren't good enough or deserving enough to reach their goals. If you are one of those who keeps saying "no" while others you trust are saying "yes" and if you have a tendency to be hard on yourself, spending some time on an assessment and sharing it with others you trust may be essential.

What is realistic for you may well include your dreams. However, while you hold on to those dreams, do some exploring of other choices as well.

Now make a list of your goals — try to have more than one and less than five — in order of preference. As you gain more knowledge of the world of dance and of your own talent, your list may change.

3. Exploring possibilities

It is important to know the world of dance — at least the part of it that relates to your interests and skills, temperament and values — if you are to have the best chance of finding a good place for yourself. Exploring possibilities and setting new goals may present an interesting challenge if you have been involved heart, mind and soul with your school (as is often required). You can do many things to prepare to explore new paths and discover new goals. Once you are aware of other possibilities, your original goal actually may appear to have been totally inappropriate — something you were led to believe you *should* aspire to, not something that evolved from inside as you grew in your own individual way.

To set new goals, you need information. It helps to become involved with the dance world in as many ways as possible. There are many ways you can do this, both on your own and with the co-operation of your school.

Get to know what is out there in as thorough a way as possible. Decide if a company is of interest to you, before you give that company the power to decide if you are of interest to it. See as many companies as possible, both local and touring. If you can't see the company perform live and it is located nearby, call or write to its office, asking if you can see some of its videos and/or watch rehearsals. If its work appeals to you and you feel up to the standard of the dancers in the company, ask if it is possible for you to take company class. Many touring companies will let you take company class, as well. Showing an interest by watching and participating is a way of being noticed, as well as a way of gaining experience and knowledge.

In groups

1. At this point, you have explored your own thoughts about the possible misinformation or lack of information that may have led to confusion about what to expect from yourself and your school as regards goals. Take time now to share your insights.

2. If you choose, first give your assessors' views on your work, then read your own assessment of yourself to at least one person whom you respect and trust. Take a deep breath and take in the feedback you get, learning what you can from it.

3. Take some time to discuss other ways in which you — individually, in groups and with the co-operation of your school — can take steps to acquire the much-needed information you may need to help you establish realistic goals.

Preparing now by becoming conscious of your abilities and desires as a dancer will help put you in touch with realistic goals.

Preparing now by reaffirming an old focus will keep energy and hope in your work.

Preparing now, while you have the time, by gaining new knowledge both of yourself and the world of dance will give you more control of your life when, next year, you may be under pressure to find work.

Part 2

expectations and realities

The aspect of making a transition into professional life that you have explored involves making ongoing personal evaluations and gathering information before you decide on a direction you'll take.

A second aspect of this transition involves clearing up misconceptions you may have concerning what happens in your life after you have chosen your direction and are working with a company.

Even though most of you have performed in student workshops, concerts, lecture-demonstrations and in professional productions as well, professional life is still seen mainly at a distance. That's why you may have developed unrealistic expectations as to exactly what that new life involves. As one dancer said when she returned from her first cross-Canada tour: "It's better than I thought and worse than I thought."

Here are a number of statements made by students about to pursue professional careers and by professional dancers a year or two past full-time training.

Before: *"After all the hard work, it will be great to be in a company."*

After: *"The first thing that I had to get used to was that I actually had longer hours, more work to do at home, more exhaustion and less social time than ever before."*

Before: *"I've managed well with injuries because I know when to take time off to recover. I'll survive in a company because I'll do the same."*

After: *"Even with most injuries, I push myself as hard as possible to never miss a performance. I'm too afraid of losing a role or of letting other people down."*

Before: *"I'm at the peak of my technical abilities now because I'm taking three classes a day. Now I just have to maintain what I have."*
After: *"At school I felt the development of my technique being guided. Now I have to take more responsibility to guide myself."*
"I need more technique than I ever had as a student. Also, you have to be warmed up all day."

Before: *"It will be great to be rehearsing all the time instead of spending so much time in class."*
After: *"Now I really wish I had that extra class every day. It's hard keeping it all together when you're so much on your own."*

Before: *"Sometimes there is so much competition in class, with everyone wanting to join the company. When I'm in a company I can relax a lot more."*
After: *"I was the best in my class, which is why I'm here now. But now I realize that I'm just one of the best along with other people who were the best in their classes. I have to set a whole new set of goals for myself."*

Before: *"Nothing could be more exciting than touring."*
After: *"Not having an accompanist play for class for five weeks was hard. I didn't expect all the long bus rides and how they would make my body feel."*
"When the floor's too hard and it's so cold you can see your breath in the air, the sponsor always says, 'but we've sold all the seats and our series will fold if you don't go on.'"

Before: *"In school I never have any problems learning rep. Since being in a company mainly involves doing rep, I know a company schedule will suit me."*

After: *"At school we spent three months learning a piece. Sometimes now I get three rehearsals."*

Before: *"I'm an independent person, and when I'm in a company, I'll go my own way."*

After: *"This is a big company, and to get to know some of the senior people you just have to get involved with them socially. Sometimes I go out drinking with someone I want to meet, even though I never did that before. I usually order what they order."*

Before: *"Finally, no more part-time jobs."*

After: *"I'm in a good modern dance company, but with 35 weeks on salary, and pretty low my first year, I still have to work part time."*

One student summed it all up in this way: *"It's cold and unromantic, but the bottom line is that I'm not paying for class anymore. I'm an employee being paid to do a job. I'm not just expected to maintain a standard, I'm expected to raise it."*

Sometimes the transition from student to performer happens relatively easily. Sometimes the change causes pressures that are hard to handle. It is unfortunate when a dancer has worked very hard for a long time and does not have the stability to deal with all these pressures of change. Not everyone with a great dance technique has the stuff to handle the ups and downs of a life in dance, both in and out of the studio. A person gains stability in many ways, one of which includes preparing, both mentally and emotionally, to deal with the immediate future. Shaping a realistic view of what to expect after your transition to company life can be helpful in this respect. The observations of the dancers quoted earlier, as well as your responses to them, should help clear up some misconceptions so that your expectations of life in a dance company are as realistic as possible.

At home and in groups

With the comments of your fellow dancers in mind, here are some questions for you to consider. They will give you a chance to think about some of the issues dancers are dealing with, often on their own. Some of these concerns may be yours right now.

1. Without your usual two or three classes a day, how will you keep improving technically?

2. What will you do if you have an injury or are so exhausted that you feel you're close to being injured?

3. What if you like your company but do not respect your director or choreographer?

4. After being the best in your class, how will you deal with being one of the best in a large company in which you may find yourself part of a chorus of 20?

5. What if someone else, new like you and no more talented, keeps getting all the good roles?

6. What if you're the chosen one?

7. What can you do to minimize the discomforts of touring?

8. How can you save money on tour?

9. How do you deal with being away from someone you love and/or count on for support?

10. What if conditions in a theatre you are asked to perform in are sub-standard?

11. How do you deal with having to share your dressing room before a performance with someone who behaves in ways that make you nervous?

12. How far will you sway from your own beliefs to gain the approval of an artist you respect? How far will you sway to fit in with your peers?

13. Do you believe in playing political or social games to get attention or to get ahead?

14. What would you say to someone who takes drugs or drinks too much because, s/he tells you:
— as an artist s/he must experience as many new sensations as possible.
— s/he needs inspiration
— s/he feels scared, nervous, bored or lonely
— s/he needs something to calm her/him down
— s/he needs something to soothe physical or emotional pain
— s/he needs energy
— s/he will feel left out because her/his friends do it.

CHAPTER 4

Part 1

auditioning

T he company audition is something most dancers will have to experience at least once during their careers. An audition can be a nerve-wracking affair as you present yourself at your most vulnerable to the judging eyes of, usually, strangers. But an audition can also be an enjoyable learning experience in which you have a chance (think of it as a free class) to explore who you are and how you've progressed.

How you feel at your audition will depend on many factors, including how desperate you are for work, how much the particular company means to you, how you define success, how good you feel about yourself and how much power you allow yourself to give to other people.

How you prepare for your audition, as well as how you react to its outcome, may be as important as the audition itself.

Here is a brief questionnaire to test your survival instinct. Any number of choices, including none, may be appropriate.

Before

1. When you hear about the audition
— Send a resumé, so the director will have an idea of who you are
— Tell other dancers who might attend something negative about the company to discourage them from going
— Find out in what style the company works and prepare in class by emphasizing qualities you believe will be required
— Go on a severe diet

2. Along with your resumé include

— A statement about why you would like to join the company

— References from some people who know your work

— An 8 x 10 headshot

— A note saying that if you are not accepted into the company, you will be happy to work in its office

3. If you are nervous

— Do some relaxation exercises or meditate

— Take drugs

— Check out the competition, finding something unattractive about each person so you'll feel better about yourself

4. Drugs can be taken

— To give you energy

— To inspire you

— To ensure that you will enjoy the audition

— None of the above

5. Wear

— Clothing that reflects the style of the company

— Simple tights and leotard, or a unitard

— A lot of warm-up clothes

— A few extra articles of clothing, wisely selected to cover body parts that you feel need a bit of camouflage

6. For good luck bring

— A pet

— A good luck charm

— Your Walkman

— Your mother

7. Arrive
— Early, to warm up
— Just in time, since the audition will provide a warm-up
— A bit late, to be noticed
— After the warm-up, since your strength is in moving
across the floor

During

8. The people watching
— Want you to do well
— Want you to do badly to make it easier to choose
— Are nervous, too, because a choice has to be made
based on knowing all of you for only a short time

9. While dancing
— Just show strong technique
— Show a personal interpretation of the material
— Show how big you can move by forcing others to the
side through the sheer power of your movement
— Show you love to dance

10. When given a variation that is confusing
— Ask questions if it is not understood
— Observe without questioning
— Go to the back, where no one will see you
— Do it wrong, but dance full out

11. When others are dancing
— Stand at the side, watch and wait
— Talk to yourself to distract the people dancing
— Mark at the side, quietly and unnoticed
— Dance full out at the side to show how much you love
dancing

After

12. If you get a call-back
— Wear the same outfit, makeup and hairstyle as you wore for the first audition
— Wear a new outfit to show your versatility
— Wear a company T-shirt to show your loyalty

13. If you get cut
— And have been cut from every audition you've ever attended, take some time to do some serious re-evaluation
— Stomp out to show how much it meant to you
— Show up for the call-back anyway, since there must have been some mistake
— Tell everyone who wasn't there how unfair it was, so it won't seem like a great loss
— Ask for another chance since you were at the back all the time
— Hate yourself because it means you're a bad dancer

14. If you get cut
— Ask the director why before you leave, since she/he owes you the truth
— Write or call later to find out why
— Come to your own conclusions
— Review your performance, learning what you can from it
— Visualize positively anything that didn't go well

15. A successful audition means
— You got the job
— You learned something about yourself
— You did your best

Part 2

taking charge of your life in dance

When students first enter a school, it is natural for them to give the responsibility of their direction to teachers, principal or director. After all, the reason for coming to the school is to absorb what it has to offer, and who better to give the information than those in charge? By the time you are finishing your last full-time year of training, the scales should have tipped a bit. Although you still need direction from the outside, you probably will survive best in the years ahead if you are by now taking more and more responsibility for yourself. As one student said, "You have to commit, not submit." It can't be said any better.

You deserve to reach your full potential. It is important to take in all the information available to you and to listen to the guidance offered by those who have more experience than you. Finally, though, you have to be the final choice maker and direction setter.

You can take control of your life in many ways so as to maximize all of your potential. The following discussion includes an outline of some of these ways, a few of which have already been explored.

1. Given all the stress of a life in dance, it is important to create for yourself a strong physical base from which you can act and react. Working on achieving or maintaining good health and making a plan by which you can save money are two lines of action that are essential.

Most dancers seem to know what is good for them in terms of nutrition, but many don't act on that knowledge. Most think it's impossible to save money in terms of how little they earn. Ask your principal or director to invite a nutritionist and/or a financial consultant to meet with you to give you the advice you need.

2. Make sure you are getting and continue to get the best possible training. "Practice makes perfect" is a misleading quote. "Perfect practice makes perfect" is better. If you and others feel you are not getting what you need from your teachers, speak to your director about your concerns.

3. Pay attention to, and respect, your own personal rhythms. Some people like to go jogging as soon as they wake up; others need two hours to get to their first cup of coffee. Some swear by hot baths, others say that only cold showers do the trick. Of course, you have a schedule to respect. But within the framework of your work day, do what you've learned is best for you. Don't go out for a big lunch with your friends if it's going to make you fall asleep an hour later. Speak up if you have been doing your best but are overly tired or injured or need a rest. It's scary to think of the show going on without you, but rest assured that it will go on without you a lot longer if you don't pay attention to danger signs, both from your body and your emotions.

4. If you plan to become an independent dancer, one who performs with a number of groups instead of performing constantly with one company, or if you are curious about this lifestyle, remember that this course is a highly respected one. How to make a full dancer's life out of the freelance reality is a good question to consider. Through your school, organize a meeting of prominent freelance dancers in your community, so they can give you advice — practical, financial and so on — so you will have a better understanding of this lifestyle and be better prepared for next year.

5. Do your best to keep a positive attitude. Learn to identify and deal with all the negatives, both those that rise from within you and those that come at you from outside. Listen to negatives at your own risk.

6. Criticism and judgment will almost always be a part of your life in dance. Learn how to use what is necessary for your progress and let go of the rest. Don't let critics manipulate your life.

7. Work on identifying and letting go of the "shoulds" and "woulds." A school may, over the years, leave you with the impression that there are certain paths that you *should* take and *would* be better off taking. Following the herd may be unwise if your own talent and potential lie in another direction.

8. Be aware of peer pressure leading you away from the course that you really believe is best for you. There are two kinds of people — the movers and the shakers, and those who are moved and shaken. Learn what you can from others and then make your own choices.

9. Do your best to be in touch with a good support system. Someone to talk with — relation, friend, lover, teacher, therapist — whether at home or on tour can help you express what might otherwise remain bottled up inside, causing you discomfort. Talking about what is bothering you may take care of the problem or it may be a good beginning. Whatever it is you have to express, make sure the person you're talking to is the right one to deal with it.

10. Keep your priorities in order and re-evaluate them from time to time. Dance will be on the top of your list, but leave room for interests and friends outside of the profession. If dance becomes the only thing in your life, you may start identifying with it and, like some dancers, feel only as good as your last class or performance. Balance is the key word here.

11. If you are unhappy with anything at your school — politics, teaching, schedules, whatever — make sure you are not reacting too personally, then speak up. Your school and its policies have never remained static. Changes have occurred during its history that make life better for you than it was for the students before you. *Initiate discussion and then speak thoughtfully and respectfully*. Sometimes it's difficult for your director or principal to know exactly what you're going through, because she/he has so many responsibilities. Saying what you feel at the right time and in the right place is one important way you can possibly bring about changes, for yourself and for those who will follow you.

12. When many students first arrive at a school, whether at the age of 8 or 18, they idealize their teachers, putting them high up on pedestals because they need to believe they are all-knowing and can give them exactly what they need. All artists, whatever their stature, naturally look to teachers all their lives for guidance. One thing that keeps dancers dancing is their hunger for new information and possibilities. So the development of a mutual trust between teacher and student is essential. It is important that the teacher/student relationship be an *equal* partnership. Leaving your teachers up on those pedestals prevents that equality, limiting the process of discovery.

Any human being or idea that is idealized and placed on a pedestal probably will come crashing down one day. Save yourself the confusion and disappointment by allowing your teachers to be human beings, with their fair share of strengths and weaknesses. If you give the power to others to shape your life and make you a dancer and your dreams (and their dreams for you) don't come true, you may feel like an innocent victim. On the other hand, when you do well, it is important to know that through the guidance of your teachers, through a learning process that is a collaboration based on mutual trust, you and your teachers share in your growth.

In groups

You have explored most of these points in past sessions. In this last meeting, review them, noting how your point of view may have changed with time. You won't need any questions to direct you, as the discussion is likely to rise out of the information quite easily. Chose the issues that concern you the most. By this time, you probably are taking more control of your life, leaving less to "the great unknown" and more to your own conscious ability to make good choices.

You are fortunate to be in touch with a process that has the possibility of enriching every aspect of your being. You are choosing a life that has goals that are stepping stones to other goals. Challenge and discovery are always there for you. The risks of your desire and courage are admirable. Taking more and more charge of your life, finding your own balance between structures and freedoms, makes movement along your own individual path more of your own responsibility, opening up the possibilities of dance and making the triumphs of creativity and energy and spirit very much your own.

Editing and design: Inprint Editorial Services
This book is also available in French